Why
Serial Killers Kill

Why
Child Molesters
Molest

I am a "psychopath" have always been one. "I wish I were sorry, but I am not." - Mark Condit, Austin bomber

What if you knew what made a serial killer a serial killer. What if you knew what made him/her kill? What would you do? What if you knew what made a child molester molest. And what if you knew how to heal them?

TABLE OF CONTENTS

You know who they are. They are the ones we can dismiss because they are the dregs of humanity. They are the most worthless parts of our society. They are the child molesters. They are the serial killers. They are the monsters.

We call them "bad" people. We say they are just murderers or sick or disgusting. They are the bottom of the barrel of society.

We label them then throw them away.

But in labeling them, removing them as humans and throwing them away we fail to understand and in so doing we are endangering every potential victim of these horrors of humanity who often by their own admission have no idea why they do what they do and little or no, according to them, control over it.

When Russell Williams, serial killer and former Air Force colonel, was asked by the police interrogator whether, if he hadn't been caught he would have kept killing he answered, "I was hoping not."

Note: Russell Williams went to a psychiatrist while he was in prison. The psychiatrist could only say, "He couldn't stop himself" but not give a reason why.   This is because psychiatrists deal with things of the adult like Freud's Defense Mechanisms and not things that happen in the very young child. They don't deal with the being in the early stages of development. Nor do they deal with the basic cognitive makeup of the baby before and directly after birth.

There are people in the world who do horrible things and sometimes not so horrible things and have no idea why they do them.

One doesn't "hope" when one has power over himself. One doesn't "Hope" to do things that are possible to do. "Hope" is a wish concerning that over which one has no control.

For the people for whom this book was written "hoping" to not do whatever it was they were prone to do was all they thought they had as Russell Williams basically stated.

Psychiatrists are at a loss to explain things as are the criminals and the police.

This book is about those who had and have no idea why they commit their crimes or act immorally. It is not for those who knew and chose wrong. It is for the criminals and for potential victims, who, it is my hope, won't become criminals or victims because what caused the crimes will now be understood.

This Book:

One year on Memorial Day a boy of 17 stood in the woods near his home with the intent to kill a jogger that was running by. He didn't know her and he didn't hate her. She was just a person and he had to kill her.

Luckily for her he failed.

In October that same boy who should have been watching videos with friends, playing baseball, maybe looking at Playboy was waiting for a ten-year-old girl to walk by to grab her. She was not so lucky and was killed by the boy.

Why?

Why was this, boy, yes, he was still a boy, spending his time standing in the woods trying to kill people he didn't know? Why did he consider himself a monster? Why was he not home doing what other boys his age were doing? Why did he need to kill?

Why?

Please be advised that this book was written for ease of understanding but will still need to be studied, contemplated and, more than anything, it will need to be applied.

In fact, in all honesty in some instances individual lines on their own will have to be contemplated to be understood.

This book is not for or about those caught up in gangs or doing what is criminal for money, revenge, ego or such things, though it may help them as well. This book is for and about persons who commit heinous crimes such as murder, child molestation and the like and do so because they are caught in a destructive situation, a destructive Thought, from which they can neither escape nor hide.

This book is about those caught in this hidden catastrophic Thought that plagues them, that sends them alone into oblivion and that is destined to destroy their lives and the lives of so many others who cross their paths. It is this Thought that causes them to do horrible things they cannot explain. It is a Thought they wish would not be so powerful. It is, a Thought they desperately wish would go away.

But without knowledge of why it is there and what it is it won't go away.

Many criminals like Russell Williams and Jeffrey Dahmer, who I am using for this book because of their extreme situations, were asked why they did the things they did. What they said was that they have absolutely no idea. They have, in addition, no idea why the Thought to kill or molest was so powerful that they risked and often lost everything including their freedom and life because of it.

The reason that the person has no idea what is going on is that the problem started in the child at an age when the child's brain was not developed enough for it to understand or remember. Also, it happened at a time when in the young brain what it Thought (yes, with a capital as all the important words in the book will have) was all it had. It happened in this basic beginning programming of the child prior to birth. Therefore, it is deep, all-encompassing and very powerful and, probably to the shock of anyone reading this, has to do with being a part of the child's "Natural State of Being"

Can it be fixed? Yes, I believe it can. Fixing the problem and saving lives is the reason for writing this book but much needs to be understood and intense work toward that understanding will have to be done.

Also, when you are done with this book either because you no longer need it or for whatever reason please, please donate it to the library or leave it at a laundromat or anywhere where someone can find it, use it and possibly save a life.

Those who wish to buy it can do so on the Internet but maybe someone will need it who has no idea they can buy it or that this book even exists so, please donate it or just leave it somewhere for them.

CHAPTER 1
Why This Book

Purpose of this chapter: To understand why this book was written.

You know who they are. They are the ones we can dismiss because they are the worse of humanity. But they are also someone's son, brother, spouse, friend, family member. Well, if the family still loves them after they find out.

The answers in this book have been used by me not only in my own everyday life for general living but in my professional life with the most difficult of students and they have never once let me down.

What I am sharing with you is the rock on which I stand and the air that I breathe. It is the reason people in my profession tell me I am so strong and they lean on me all the time. It is this information that I am happy to share with you.

This book started decades ago when I first met someone who was caught in a terrible overpowering Thought and I watched it eat at him until there was nothing left. I watched helplessly as it destroyed my friend but could do nothing. I learned later about other people who got caught in a Thought that was destined to ruin their lives. I wanted to do something about it then but had neither the strength nor the answers at that time.

When I watched the story of Russell Williams on the television it broke my heart because I knew the tragedy caused by being under the control of such a powerful horrible Thought could have been prevented and I knew it was nearly the same tragedy that could have been prevented with my friend years before. I knew that what had happened to my friend, though in a very different light since not all destructive Thoughts are the same, had happened in a different aspect again.

I knew that what happened to my friend decades before was in essence what happened to Russell Williams and other serial killers and child molesters. This time, however, I was determined to do something because now I could.

Russell Williams was a highly decorated Colonel in the Canadian Air Force. In January 2010 he commanded the Canadian Forces Base in Trenton, the largest and busiest Air Force Base in Canada. He was a decorated military pilot who had flown Canadian Air Forces VIP aircraft for dignitaries such as Queen Elizabeth II, Prince Phillip and the Governor General and Prime Minister of Canada.

But that was in January. In February 2010, he was known throughout his world in Canada as a rapist, thief, possible pedophile, cross-dresser and murderer. Pictures of him in women's undergarments were sprawled across the Canadian media. You can and should Google it.

And his wife of nine years and his best friend from college were both left in a state of shock, horror, devastation and colossal incomprehensible confusion.

So, what happened to all of these people who do all these crazy and at times not only crazy but crazy and cruel things? Almost all of them have one thing in common. They have no idea why they did what they did. They had no idea why they thought as they thought. And they had no idea why they couldn't stop.

Ask Russell Williams why he did what he did and why he had to break into women's homes risking his entire life and career to get their underwear instead of buying them at Sears and he will shrug and indicate he has no idea. And he really had and has no idea.

Jeffrey Dahmer was a man who killed and ate seventeen men and boys that he lured to his room with the promise of a sexual relationship. He was known as the Milwaukee Cannibal. His father, a normal middle aged caring father, stated that except for a divorce they were a normal, typical family. His stepmother cried for both Jeffrey and the victims. Approximately three years later Jeffrey was killed in prison by being beaten with a pipe by other inmates. I was so sad because he could have helped me so much.

If you could have asked Jeffery Dahmer why he felt compelled to eat the people he brought home rather than have a relationship with them, he would have told you, like Russell Williams, he had no idea. He said that he thought about it many times and wished he knew so he could have fixed it and lived his life normally as it was supposed to have been lived. But I know why.

They and people like them have absolutely, positively no idea why they did what they did…none whatsoever. And I know they have thought about it incessantly. A friend of Dennis Rader, the BTK killer, once said, "His mind was a thousand miles away".

But I can tell you why. I can tell you what happened to drive these people to do the things they did. It was not a desire. It was not a want. It was a very, very deep need and it was there before birth.

There has been, throughout the centuries right up to this day, an intense mystery to these situations that compels family, friends, law enforcement and even psychologists to say, "Just tell me why. Why did you do this to people you didn't even know? Why did you do this to people who did nothing to you? Why did you do this at all?"

To try to make sense of it all the psychologists, psychiatrists and others who should have some sort of answer simply say the person is a "evil person" or a "pedophile" or a "serial killer" or a "rapist' a "murderer" and so on. The people are labeled as if that explains things. They say there are human beings and there are pedophiles, serial killers, rapists and murderers. That's all.

That is what they are.

But that is not the truth. Not in my opinion, anyway.

Hope, Healing and Wow:

I searched the Internet not for anyone in particular but for a sample of a person who simply killed victims and took no other action upon them. I was looking for example of killing only to explain how it was done for the purpose of taking one's humanity.

I came across a video on YouTube and watched it not knowing what I would find. In this video I had the great pleasure of seeing in an interview the healed serial killer, David Berkowitz.

I lived in New York where he killed so many years before and studied him a bit then. I knew how dazed and arrogant he looked when he was arrested and how much he smirked and how much he lied to police. My memory of him was so different from the man in the interview.

I know that he was really healed because first of all he had no reason to lie at this point in his life since he will never be released from prison, second because I knew what being healed would look like, and third and most importantly because his affect, which was really off in his killing days, was now perfectly, beautifully normal if not better than normal.

During his killing days he called himself "Son of Sam' as he drove around the streets of New York City and Long Island around the year 1977 shooting people in the head as they sat in their cars or walked into their homes. He killed six people, injured seven others and terrorized the city.

The topic turned to being forgiven when David said, "I know God has forgiven me even though others may never forgive me" As it turns out before Mrs. Moskowitz, mother of one of David's victims, Stacy Moskowitz, died she wrote to him and said she forgave him.

A question from one interviewer: David, have you been able to forgive yourself?

He answered: "There was a long time of struggle where I couldn't forgive myself and I went through a lot of pain during that time period. One day a minister was giving a sermon from the book of Micah the prophet and he talked about God taking all your sins and throwing them into the sea of forgetfulness never to be remembered anymore and as he was speaking I felt like God's spirit …just …bloom in me at that moment and God was reaching out to me and saying David, your sins are forgiven. David, I have completely forgiven you. I love you. I want you to know that and right then and there it was like a light went off inside me. I knew from that moment my sins were completely forgiven."

As far as the old David is concerned: "It's like another life that I don't ever recognize any more."

Seeing the video of David Berkowitz gave me the hope that I can explain what happened and make you understand. It was so refreshing.

This book was written not only to help the person who may commit the crimes but for their victims and all the friends and family involved. This book was not written to excuse or lessen the damage done, remove responsibility or in any way devalue the victims. This book was written to prevent any more heartache, pain and death.

I will explain everything you need to know and then apply it to the individual cases of Russell Williams, Jeffrey Dahmer and others. Read this book slowly, absorb the deep concepts and apply them to life. This will give you the understanding you will need.

.

CHAPTER 2
About Me

Purpose of this chapter: To understand me in order for you to trust in my words.

How I know things:

In order for you to understand it will help for you to have a little information about me and my history.

I am a Special Education teacher; or rather I was before I retired. And I was a special education teacher from the day I was born. I taught the most bizarre students and considered the most confusing to the general public to be a fun challenge. Most of the time, I understood them easily.

The schools where I worked marveled at my ability to work with those children and had tremendous respect for me though I thought of my ability as simply a part of me and nothing particularly special or unique.

My specialty was Child Development and my degree is in Child Development and Human Relations though that college taught education was not the basis of my knowledge but to support a lot of what I already knew from years working with students and studying them directly.

Understanding people was always my goal, my absolute and only goal. And understanding often came about in the smallest most minute particles of the question. When the question was unanswerable it was because it was too large or general and had to be broken down into many smaller questions with many smaller answers.

I had no loyalty to any philosophy or particular person. If the theory stated by any professional proved correct in my work I kept that concept. Sometimes I would hold to one idea of a particular psychiatrist or psychologist or philosopher and let go of all else. That gave me only an answer to work with which was always best.

I wanted only Truth and did not care where it came from. I needed sensible reliable answers.

I studied Child Development and genetic epistemology, which is the study of how knowledge structures work This in relation to the mind of the child was fascinating to me.

I studied how children form their knowledge structures in the world and the origin of things concerning the child's growing mind and the cognitive process that made the child develop into an adult.

The research that I studied brought about, for me, the understanding of the depth and progression of the growing Mind of the child and his research proved true and usable in my classroom.

I was a person who had to know why my entire life. Even when I was taught how to drive a stick shift car I could not learn until it was explained to me how the gears worked. Then it was easy.

The things I learned concerning cognitive development in the child have proven to be true and have worked time and again in my career in working with the most severe of behaviorally or cognitively handicapped students. Because of this proof I call it not a theory but a fact, an answer.

But it wasn't this particular research that was so important to me and this research will not necessarily bring about understanding of the serial killer and child molester. What it revealed was that there is a real and planned sequence of development that is automatically followed for the child to grow.

Thought and Mind hold the key to understanding those for whom and about whom this book was written and understanding how that Mind works is essential.

In addition to the progressive development of the child, I have studied psychiatry and the basic make-up of mankind in general. My interest included learning that took place before and directly after birth.

In addition, I have teaching certifications in multiple states and am an author and inventor.

I hope this convinces you that I truly know what I am saying and gives you faith in my qualifications in understanding concerning what you are about to read.

I will be discussing:
- Stages of Physical and Mental development showing how the being's growth is preplanned

- Mental development and the role of Thought and Mind

- Concept and Action Thoughts

- Memory

- Thoughts implanted in the Child as its "Natural State of Being".

- How the Mind works

- The entity called the "self"

- What went wrong

- Why it is not remembered by the person

- Why they are driven

- "Hell-Thoughts" that make people kill or molest

- What happened

- The cure

I am going to talk about why there is no memory of what happened.

I am going to explain the natural "Thought" makeup of the child prior to birth and how it forms the "Natural State of Being" in the child.

I will explain the difference between the serial killer and the child molester.

I will explain the "Thought" process in the development of the child, the "Thought" process of memory and the "Thought' process that is the "Natural State of Being" and I will put all three of these things together to give you an understanding of the make up of the human being.

Then I will explain what happened and what went wrong to make a person a serial killer or child molester.

After that I will present what I believe to be the cure.

PART I

THE MAKING OF THE PERFECT BEING

CHAPTER 3

Planned and Programmed

The Purpose of this chapter: To show you how the child is preplanned physically and cognitively from the very start.

Congratulations we are going to make a baby.

Sorry, it will not be done the typical fun way.

I want to start at the very, very beginning to explain to you what happened to those who became serial killers or child molesters. Bear with me, there is a point to this way of explaining what happened.

Physically:

If we start physically from the very beginning we have the naturally planned sequence of the sperm swimming through the cervix and the fallopian tubes toward the egg by use if its long tail. As it gets closer to the egg the planned sequence is that the head of the sperm hardens to force entry into the egg. The sperm meets the egg and enters causing the next part of the sequence to be that the egg closes up so that the other billion or so sperms are not able to enter so the mother does not give birth to a billion babies at once.

Once the fertilized the egg splits and splits the cells do not simply reproduce haphazardly just for the purpose of making more and more cells. There is a set plan for the cells to each one become a cellular piece of a particular larger thing like a lung or a heart and so on. If there was not a set plan, we would simply be a blob of cells on the floor.

So why am I telling you this?

Cognitively:

First one needs to know that the word cognitive simply means mental learning or just learning.

I want you to understand that just as there is a preset plan in the physical development of the child both before birth and after there is a cognitive plan, sequence, progression in the child both before birth and after.

From the first day of conception to birth, and, of course after, there is a preset plan for physical development and for cognitive development in the child. At some time between conception and birth the Mind of the child is being programmed as well. This programming holds the key to why serial killers kill and child molesters molest and why psychiatrists and such types of professionals have no understanding of serial killers or child molesters and why the serial killers and child molesters feel the need to do what they do.

Please note that the word Thought has been and will be capitalized in this book. The reason for that is that you have to realize for the understanding of this book that a Thought is an actual thing or entity. Each cell has a Thought as part of it so it knows what to do.

For instance, cells like white blood cells, are given the job of cleaning the body of foreign objects and will work aggressively to do so. It does not have Thoughts to do anything but clean nor does it have the same Thought to beat in unison as does a heart cell or make other cells as with bone marrow.

Other important words, like Mind, will also be capitalized for importance and the concept that it is an actual thing or entity as well.

Now, the Mind that is connected to the physical vehicle called the brain is made of a unified group of Thoughts for the baby to keep and use to grow. There are Thoughts of cause and effect; Thoughts that allow the child to adjust to unusual situations; Thoughts that allow the child to change its Mind about a Though. There are Thoughts that have the child attempt to learn; Thoughts to be inquisitive; Thoughts for memory; there is the Thought that tells the baby it has a self; there is the Thought that tells the baby it is worthy and loved; there is the Thought that shows it as a human entity in the world and so on.

As with the physical plan there is a cognitive plan, a Mind plan. The plan for the building of the physical aspect of the child is perfect as is the plan for the building of the mental aspect of the child.

Thoughts that make up the Mind are like the cells of the body. There are probably hundreds of thousands if not millions and they work in unison as the hundreds of thousands if not millions of cells of the body work in unison.

The cells of the body build a body while the Thoughts of the Mind build a "self".

Thoughts are organized in a specific way to build upon each other just as cells of the body are planned to build upon each other.

In the programmed Thought dealing with the physical realm, the baby is programmed to suck when its lips are touched and later to move its head to find the nipple etc. That is a mental or Thought program. Without that programmed Thought in the Mind of the baby it would not be able to eat or live.

The child will cry when it feels hunger or something uncomfortable. This is the way the child talks. It is cognitively programmed to do this. The child will sleep a lot at first in order for its brain to grow and adapt to its new world. It is physically programmed to do this. Later as the child grows it begins to use its mental capabilities more and more which are also in its programming.

The child is programmed to explore in order to learn. In its mental learning process the child is programmed and that programming goes through predetermined stages of development just as a computer goes from one file to another until the process is complete.

I have decided that the best way to describe the planned and planted Thoughts is to use the analogy of a computer because the child is "Programmed"… just like a Computer is programmed.

In the programmed Thought progression where the child learns to grow known as Child Development, which I have studied including prior to birth programming, the Thoughts build upon each other to grow just as the cells of the body build upon each other to grow to produce a physical adult.

In this day and age people are well aware of the way computers work. People know what it means to "boot up" a computer. They know what it means to need files to build upon each other.

Therefore, I am using the analogy of how the computer works to explain the beginning of cognitive life in a human child and the process that needs to be understood in order to begin the journey to understanding and healing of the serial killer and child molester.

Like a computer, the child boots up. It goes through a complete boot up procedure just like a computer. You could call it, and I see it as, booting up the human operating system.

The first boot up action of the child's cognitive operating system is to start the child off and allow it to process and store memories with which it can grow.

Like a computer if the computer had no means to store bits of data in memory the computer would be useless. Therefore, the child needs to have a place to store data in its memory as well.

The difference, and this is most important in understanding the serial killer and child molester, is that the computer simply places all data in its bank then uses that data to build the next step. This is why the computer will sometimes crash if a file, like a dll file is missing.

(To get off the track a little bit one could say the human dll file in the serial killer and child molester is missing or better said dormant and of course they have no idea just as a person looking at a CD could not tell if the dll file is missing)

The one thing the child does not have in its memory bank is that it can think and that there is something other than what it is living. The child's memory bank for the first years of life is filling very fast with Thought things of life that are mostly related to the physical (like how to grab and crawl) and its awareness of being able to think and know there is more to the world is not there.

The child is not aware that it can "think" therefore all that it learns is not something it is aware of learning. If the child learns fear or if the child learns insecurity it will not be able to recall having learned those things because it has not learned that it can think and it does not at that time know anything different.

In the first years, memory is underdeveloped or undeveloped. The baby at this First Memory Stage does not know it can think therefore it cannot "realize" it "Thought" something. If the Thought that it likes itself or is a human being was not there the child wouldn't know.

If such a thing happened it would be not only unrealized but what was missing would be unable to be remembered. It would seem as if it was simply part of the child's personality and understanding this is very, very important when trying to understand the serial killer or child molester.

If a Thought was damaged or missing before birth or at this First Memory Stage it would seem as if it was always gone which causes the serial killer to say that he is a monster from birth.

Remember though, things can go wrong in both the physical and mental worlds as the child progresses through life as we all know, the plan itself is perfect.

CHAPTER 4
Thought and Mind

Purpose of this chapter: To understand that there are Preset connected Concept Thoughts and Action Thoughts that are placed in the child's Mind from the very beginning.

Physically, in addition to the preset plan that each cell of the body has a particular purpose, each cell also has to act upon that purpose. A heart cell needs to beat and it needs to do so in unison with other heart cells for the heart to work as an organ.

If the heart cell knew it had to beat but did not do so or have the Thought to do so, the being would not be alive.

The cells of the lungs need to know that they are to move the lungs up and down to a particular rhythm in order for the lungs to pump air into the body. But knowing to do so and doing it are not the same. The cells of the lungs have to know what their job is and they have to actually have the Thought to do that job.

The same is, of course, true of all cells of the body.

Therefore, each cell has two "Thought" related parts. Each cell has to know what it is to do and each cell has to know to do it. These are two different Thoughts connected to each other within each physical cell and each cognitive Thought in the Mind.

The body physically holds the cells that work in unison with each of them knowing their job and each having the Thought that they are to do their job. The Mind, as well, cognitively holds the Thoughts that work in unison each of them knowing their job and each having the Thought of doing their job as well.

The cells in the body each have Concept Thoughts that tell the cell what to do and Action Thoughts that tell the cell to do it. There are Thoughts in the Mind that each have Concept Thoughts that tell the Thought what to do and Action Thoughts that tell it to do it.

And as I said the Thought part of knowing what to do I call the "Concept Thought" and the Thought part of actually doing it I call the "Action Thought". And these two parts are in every cell and every Thought in the Mind.

I discussed the body for the purpose of understanding the functions of the cells having to both know their jobs and know to act out their jobs.

Now I will talk about the Mind and its story.

The Mind in the child is the holder of Thoughts that were placed in it from before birth. It is a container, you may say, that holds all it cognitively needs to live in the world and to use with the body it was given and it communicates to the body through the brain and other parts.

Each and every separate Thought placed in the child for it to grow is made up of a Concept Thought and an Action Thought. The Concept Thoughts and Action Thoughts are connected unless something goes wrong.

Let's say the baby is hurting because it is hungry. If the baby simply was hungry and hurting and wasn't already programmed with the Concept Thought to cry to alleviate the problem and programmed with the Action Thought to take action using that Concept, it would not cry. It would simply lay there and hurt.

If the baby was hurting and had the Concept Thought to cry to alleviate the hurt but did not have the Action Thought added to that Concept Thought that action must be taken, it would just lay there and hurt.

If the baby was hurting and did not have the Concept Thought to cry to alleviate the hurt but did have the Action Thought that action must be taken, it again would just lay there and hurt or do what it knows which may be to kick or roll around.

These two scenarios are so important to know when understanding the serial killer or child molester.

So, for every single Concept Thought there must be, and is, an Action Thought connected to that Concept Thought or the Concept Thought would just be there dormant like an unpowered computer simply holding information.

Every Concept Thought must have an Action Thought connected to it, no matter how small the concept, for it to be used even if the only use for that Concept Though is to realize it (Action) or accept it (Action) or understand it (Action) or remember it (Action).

You need to understand that Mind is not brain. They are completely different. Mind is as real as the brain but it is not what one would say made of matter. The brain is simply a vehicle for the Mind to be able to use the body.

Once the Concept Thought is realized (Action) it is placed in memory (Action). There the Concept Thought stays the same but to recall from memory becomes the Action Thought. The Concept Thought does not have to become realized. It simply has to be recalled. Recalling from memory becomes the Action Thought connected to the Concept Thought.

Just to make it clear this book deals with "Thought" and only "Thought" or "Mind" not brain.

It is because of the fact that the Concept Thought and Action Thought work together and that things can go wrong in that area that many serial killers kill and child molesters molest.

CHAPTER 5
Early, Deep Concept Thoughts

The purpose of this chapter: to get an idea of the depth and understanding of the early Concept and Action Thoughts

Now you can believe that the Thoughts that are placed in the child before birth are put there at that time to simply become activated at the time specified in its preplanned programming or you can believe the Thoughts are put there later.

I believe they are put there before birth and simply are activated at the proper age per preprogramming. This would explain child prodigies.

In the first of the stages of Thought progression one of the Concept Thoughts was used at the ages from 0-2 years. In this stage the child learns "that they exist separately from the objects and people around them" and it seems unthinkable that this Thought has to be placed in the child at all but it surely does.

Now remember that along with Concept Thoughts Action Thoughts are required. So here the child has acquired the Concept Thought that it "exists separately from the objects and people around" but that Concept Thought needs an Action Thought and that Action Thought is to realize the Concept Thought. In other words, the child applies the Concept of being separate from the objects and people around it meaning that is now a physical "self". That realization and its use is the Action.

So, for better understanding I wanted to give you an example of the Concept Thoughts and Action Thoughts related to how we learn. I will be explaining one of the Thoughts that is part of the cognitive process that is used to take in new information. I will also explain Concept Thought and Action Thought and how they relate.

In later chapters I will show you the Concept Thought and Action Thought that went wrong in the case of the serial killer and the Concept Thought and Action Thought that went wrong in the case of the child molester.

First the child has a Thought that it thinks to be true, an already learned Thought.

Then the child has to take in new information and incorporate it into its already learned Thoughts in order to grow. This process has a name and you can study it in those terms in the last pages of this book but for now we will simply study it as a Thought that has to adjust a bit since that is what it really is.

For instance, that a horse may have stripes but it's still a horse would require a person to adjust its already learned Thought a bit to assimilate the new information.

But sometimes the new information does not fit into the already learned Thought so the child has to make an adjustment in its Thought for the new information.

The Mind has to modify what was previously Thought to accommodate the new information into a new Thought.

In other words, this is the process that was set in place to change your Mind and learn new things.

It is the way we learn a new Thought.

So, let's go through it again.

First the child has the already realized Concept Thought of what a horse is in its Mind because it had been taught that that is a horse.

The Concept Thought was that the word horse refers to the object of a horse. The Action Thought was the placement of that Concept as being a horse in the child's memory for later recall.

Then the child sees a zebra. It thinks that it, too, is a horse mainly because it looks like one and that is already the remembered Concept Thought in the child's Mind so it adjusts a little bit. The Concept Thought is that that object, though a bit different, is a horse. The Action Thought is that though it is a bit different, it is a horse. It is a horse with stripes to the child.

Someone says, "That's not a horse. It's a zebra. See the stripes?"

The child now has a new Concept Thought and has to "accommodate" (Action Thought) that the previous remembered Concept Thought (schema) in this instance is incorrect and that that was not a horse.

The child then has to change (Action Thought) its previous Concept Thought that this is a zebra. It uses the Action Thought of changing its Mind about the old information to make it new information.

The new information becomes a new Concept Thought that this is a zebra and that Concept is placed in memory (Action Thought).

Now in the child's Mind there is the Thought of a horse and the Thought of a zebra.

The Action Thought connected to the Concept Thought is now not to realize something but to remember it. A child does not have to realize it can walk as the Action Thought because it will remember it can walk. So, the Action Thought is to remember or recall.

And that's how we learn.

Now here is the adult version:

There was a woman who had a brother-in-law. Every time her brother-in-law came over, he brought a bouquet of flowers and kissed her on the cheek and asked how she was doing. The schema or already believed Thought is that he is a really nice guy.

One day a neighborhood teenager and her brother-in-law were helping her with a project when the brother-in-law looks out the window then suddenly leaves.

She continues with her project thinking little of it though it was odd then gets a call that her neighbor's car was stolen. She remembers that she saw her brother-in-law driving the exact same car very fast down the street.

She adjusts her thoughts. "Hmmm isn't it funny that they both have the same car?" In other words, the woman tries to make sense of what she just saw using what she already believed to be true that the brother-in-law was a nice guy.

The brother-in-law returns to the woman and the teenager with a different car and blames the teenager for the neighbor's stolen car which the woman knows that was not the case and she realizes that the brother-in-law is purposely lying and probably stole the car.

Now she has a new Concept Thought that her brother-in-law is not really a nice guy and she has to realize that that is true (Action Thought).

Now she has a new Thought concerning her brother-in-law that she has placed in her memory bank.

That is also how we learn as adults provided we don't get stuck in the Assimilating (psychologist Jean Piaget) step over and over again which Freud would call denial! Just kidding...sort of!

There are three very important points that you will find completely ridiculous to mention but are very important points to know and remember.

The first very important point is that just as the baby cannot decide it will not suck or cry, the child cannot say, "I have decided not to think today or have that particular thought." It cannot decide which of the developmental processes it will not use.

The second very important point is that it does not know and has absolutely no clue these things are happening.

The third very important point is that the child at that time does not have the brain capacity to make decisions in its programming. It has no choice but to do what it is programmed to do early in its life.

These three points may seem to you to be common sense and of no value but I can assure you they are of the upmost importance when understanding this book and what happened in the cases of Russell Williams, Jeffrey Dahmer and others.

These processes in the boot up of the child are ingrained in the child. I have to stress to you that these processes are deeply, deeply ingrained and are as deep as the cells are ingrained in the body. They are part of the child's Mind and need to be seen as such just as the cells are part of a body or the cement blocks part of a building. They are like the cells, the atoms, to the body they are the basic structure of the mental part of the child.

This information does not have to be memorized or deeply understood. The purpose of knowing about the Thoughts placed in the child as it grows is for one reason and one reason only. It is not to use it to understand the serial killer or child molester but to understand that there is a lot of deep Thought being planted in that little Mind for that little brain to use. And it is purposeful, planned and timed.

CHAPTER 6
Memory

Because memory plays such a very, very important part in the problem concerning serial killers and child molesters I have made this a chapter on its own. Memory and lack thereof holds the key to a large part of the situation and understanding of what happened in the case of serial killers and child molesters.

There are many Thought programs going on simultaneously in a growing child. Some deal with learning as in the case of the discoveries of Psychologist Piaget. Some deal with morality and memory.

The early child is governed by the "pleasure principle" and its behavior is based on pleasure with no consideration for reality or the feelings of anyone else. It is the only mental-moral capacity in this area that a child has when it is born. It sucks to please itself and relieve the feeling of hunger though it may be painful to the mother. It cries though it wakes the whole house. A young child will take another child's cookie and not think a thing of it.

This is an actual "stage" of development. In this First Memory Stage the child's behavior is unconscious and impulsive. It is the pleasure only and the "I want it now" attitude. This stage was called by one teacher "outrageously stupid".

I want you to remember back to when you were one year old and tell me what your favorite food was. Or maybe what your favorite toy was. Maybe you had a favorite pajama you liked to wear to bed.

Can't do it? Probably not.

Memory develops slowly and something what happened to cause tremendous damage would probably not be remembered or even realized if it happened at a very young age. The younger the age of trauma the less chance of remembering it.

In addition, the younger the age of trauma the more it will be all encompassing because there were no prior thoughts to counter the traumatic thought. There would have been no memory of how it was before so that Thought would have been everything. There would have been nothing else.

Due to lack of history and because there was nothing in memory already that Thought would have been all the person would know. It would be everything and the only thing.

This is again why serial killers and child molesters have no idea why they do what they do.

(Please be advised that this first stage of memory development has a professional name and is a part of the psychology world. This book deals with Thoughts but if you care to understand from that point of view you can read about it in the last pages of this book.)

CHAPTER 7
The Natural State of Being

The purpose of this chapter: a doctor cannot fix a body without knowing how a normal body should function just as one cannot fix a psyche without knowing how a normal psyche should function. Therefore, in both cases one has to know how the physical or cognitive being is made which is its "Natural State of Being".

One of the most important things I could teach you is about a person's, every person's, mental, "Natural State of Being".

I am going to try to explain at first the "Natural State of Being" using the analogy of the cells of the body.

The plan for the cells of the body to do what they should is predetermined and fixed. Everyone in their perfect physical state has a "Natural State of Being" or a "Natural State of (Physical) Being" of one head, two arms, one torso, two legs, ten fingers, one heart and so on. The plan for those cells is fixed for everyone barring something going wrong. But there is the fixed predetermined, preset plan in physical cell development.

The "Natural State of Being" in the mental or cognitive situation consists of a multitude of Concept Thoughts and Action Thoughts that are preplanned and placed in the Mind of the child before birth or after birth and continue until or maybe through adulthood.

The Thoughts that make up the "Natural State of Being" are completely unknown to the child and are placed prior to the child having the ability to remember them.

Since eating is a "Natural" thing then hunger to have to eat is a "Natural State of Being". And this "Natural State of Being" for food can drive someone to do unloving and strange things.

The hunger for the mental aspects of life that should have been placed in the child and working in its early stages of life is a hunger due to its "Natural State of Being" and that hunger or need can drive someone to do unloving and strange things as well.

The Concept Thought to be independent, for example, or the desire to be liked, the need for friendship and relationships, the need to "be a person" are all "Natural States of Being." And there are so very many more.

The Concept Thoughts linked to the Action Thoughts are the "Natural State of Being". When the Concept Thought is blocked and the concept is unfulfilled in the Mind of the child there becomes a need and a void that drives the person to do bizarre and unloving things to fill what is unfulfilled.

It is the Action Thought that makes the serial killer and child molester do what they do as it is fights to fulfill the job of the Concept Thought which cannot be fulfilled because it is blocked or stopped.

We will be dealing in this book with the Concept Thought and Action Thought, memory, and the "Natural State of Being" to explain what happened concerning the serial killer and child molester.

CHAPTER 8

Mind: Speed, Depth and the Terrible Timing

The purpose of this chapter: To show you a few more important aspects of the Mind

The Speed of Thought:

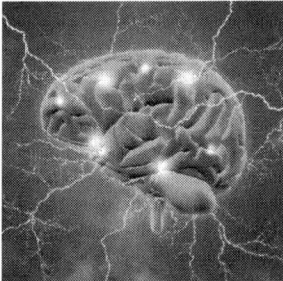

*

"With the speed of lightning" is the best way to describe how fast the mind works or maybe even that is way too slow.

And with that incredible speed not only does the person remember and use the Thoughts it has but the Thoughts communicate to produce an action or a new thought for the child to keep all within nanoseconds.

In order to do all the things we have to do, like walk as we zip our jackets, acknowledge our cold fingers, decide which way to go, walk around a hole, all the while thinking of what we want to buy for someone's birthday and where to buy it and whether that person already has that item, our minds have to work at lightning speed.

How fast the mind works is incredible especially when you think of all it has to hold while thinking of the next thing it needs to add as it assimilates, accommodates and builds schemas.

If you think of drinking a cup of coffee you can't even imagine the number of different movements and judgments you have to make with each sip. Below you will find just a very, very small list.

You have to:
Look at the cup
Send a message to your hand to grab it
Open your hand the right amount
Judge where the cup is
Place your finger in the handle of the cup
Close your hand the proper amount
Squeeze the proper amount
Lift slowly
Adjust your grip when you pick it up
Acknowledge where your mouth is
Lift it to your mouth
Place it at the proper speed toward your mouth

Judge the proper place to place it without looking
Place it at the proper place on your mouth
Perch your lips to make a seal on the cup
Lift the cup at the proper speed
Lift the cup to the proper angle
Stop lifting when the liquid gets to your lips
Sip the fluid
Judge when to stop sipping
Swallow
Lower the cup

This is a list that is by far not all inclusive of the Thoughts and actions taken to simply take a drink from a cup and in addition the person drinking is at the same time thinking and possibly talking and whatever else including using assimilation and accommodation and schema making.

The point is that Thoughts race through our minds at an incredible rate of speed in order to allow us to function throughout the day. Thoughts already in our consciousness come to us so fast we don't realize they are happening.

That speed is often the reason why habits are so hard to break and violence in some people can be so spontaneous. But if we didn't think at such an incredible rate of speed we couldn't walk or talk and certainly do both at the same time while thinking of where we parked the car and that we shouldn't have worn these shoes.

According to studies it is suggested that the conscious mind processes about 2,000 bits per second while the subconscious mind processes 400 billion bits per second.

Thoughts that don't require new schema (new Thoughts) to be built are most often automatic and unconscious. They can cause an action or a second thought that is so fast that we don't know it's there. It is very important to know this.

Remember the thoughts throughout the day change one right after another. People often think of things they think in much too broad of a concept. Thoughts are small and quick and thousands of Thoughts that happen in the day happen in a nanosecond and leave in a nanosecond as well. We need to be introspective and acknowledge the Thoughts we have throughout the day. We need to be vigilant to be aware of the tremendous number of Thoughts we think each day or maybe be vigilant of each moment.

Depth of Thought

Before you read this, I strongly urge you to watch the movie <u>Sybil</u> staring Sally Field. Sybil is the true story of a woman with multiple personalities and her journey to healing. She lived through horrendous things and survived. But the reason for watching the movie is to understand the depth of the Mind.

The movie should be watched in the dark to get the full effect of what happened with Sybil and the deep, dark journey into her psyche. This will give you an idea what I am trying to convey here and how deep the despair could be.

The Mind is like a deep dark cave where the person is completely alone except for maybe God if they are of that persuasion.

If you sit and think quietly you will realize the depth of your own mind and the quietness of your own thoughts.

We all know it. We all experience the aloneness and solitude; the darkness that is our mind. If you sit alone and think you will feel your mind going into its deepest canyons

Deep and dark and all encompassing

In that deep dark cave of the mind lies the "program" to fulfill personal needs of the being. In that deep dark cave of the mind lies the "program" to grow in morality and in memory as choices of the being are made.

In that deep dark cave of the Mind lies the "program" to form thoughts containing knowledge (schemas) and to hold those Thoughts that the child has already learned.

In that deep dark cave of the Mind you are alone.

Terrible Timing

The reason this is called Mind: Speed, Depth and the Terrible Timing is because it deals with the Mind and its speed and depth and the terrible timing of the Concept Thought that went unfulfilled at a time when memory was undeveloped.

The Mind is made up of a countless number of Concept Thoughts that are linked to Action Thoughts that are incredibly fast and incredibly deep and were planted in the Mind prior to birth to be activated before or during the First Memory Stage when memory was not able to remember and there were no memories to rely on to counter the memory.

CHAPTER 9
The Self

Purpose of this chapter: to understand that the self is an actual thing and it is in the "self" Concept where things went wrong.

The self is a live self-contained entity, which means it is an actual thing of distinct and independent existence, that is made up of things of the Mind. It is individual and separate from the rest of the world.

As time goes on the "self" gets more things added to it.

Personality, choices, principle, things learned and so on become part of that "self". Persona, character, personality, psyche, soul, spirit and so on are also part of that "self". The "self" is real. Though it may not be able to be seen it exists as a whole actual thing. It encompasses all the things that are the person except the body. It holds it together like the body holds the cells to make them function as a complete unit.

The "self" functions as a complete unit.

The "self" is an actual thing.

The body is the vehicle for the "self".

It is a piece of the "self" that is missing in the situation concerning the serial killer.

The "Natural State of Being" is what the child is made of in its programmed Mind and the child has no control over this "Natural State of Being" nor should it.

The Thoughts that make up the 'Natural State of Being' along with the persons personality, choices and such make up the "self".

Those who do not have the Thought concept of their "human entity" in the world will have a particular disorder. Those who do not have the Thought concept of their "identity' in the world will have a different disorder. Those who do not have the Thought concept of their social placement in the world will have a different disorder.

The "self" is like a cocoon where all is encapsulated. But it is a cocoon of Concept Thoughts and Action Thoughts that are connected and those Thoughts use the body.

It was suggested I give you a visual of the situation so here goes. I hope this will help.

Picture a circle. In that circle is the word Mind. Coming at that circle are Thoughts that look like tens of thousands of rays of sunlight

Then picture that same circle filled with all the sunlight it is supposed to be filled with. That is the "self". That is the normal human person who has a hard time understanding the serial killer or child molester. Though darkness may fall on the outside that is the makeup of most people.

Now picture the circle again as in the first paragraph above and in that circle is the word Mind. Coming at that circle are Thoughts that look like tens of thousands of rays of sunlight but there is a huge dark spot.

How big is the spot? How confused does it make the self? How much does the self need what should be in that spot? How much does the darkness fight to get its light?

Unless we live it, we don't know.

Oh, and what will fix it? Of course, the light.

PART II

WHAT WENT WRONG

CHAPTER 10
Unlocking the Mystery

"It is the mystery of mysteries that will never be solved."

No, it isn't.

When killers kill they do so for various reasons. It could be out of a sense of justice or entitlement as with those who thought they were stolen from. It could be out of a sense of thinking they are doing the right thing for a place in history as the angel killer who killed the elderly in a nursing home.

Killing could be for money as the killer who killed only wealthy people that can be lured. It could be for power and control. It could be out of anger and blame. It could be for revenge. It could be for misguided religious, family, or patriotic reasons, or simple attention or pride.

Those killings can be explained with logic and need to be dealt with through self-examination for motive. But what we are concerned with in this book is those whose actions cannot be explained away using common sense reasoning.

What this book is about is killing of those to whom the serial killer has no connection, or ill will of any kind. It is someone who kills due to internal issues making them need to kill.

What we are dealing with are child molesters who do not molest because they simply feel they are the same age as the victim or for any such sensible reason but to satisfy a much deeper need.

Labels galore

Psychiatrists, forensic professionals, police will say it is a mystery.

Those in the psychiatry field will give diagnosis after diagnosis without a reason why. My instructor in Abnormal Psychology once said that if you give it a name you make it real.

Jeffrey Dahmer said he finally understood when the doctors gave a name to what he "had" that made him a killer. But the name does not explain "why". Nor does it show how to heal the person. For Jeffrey it removed the guilt a bit but no healing occurred.

Jeffrey was diagnosed with sexual paraphelias (which means sexual interest in atypical things) including necrophilia (which means sexual attraction to corpses), cannibalism (which means sexual attraction when eating people), exhibitionism (which means sexual attraction when showing his genitals to unsuspecting people), pedophilia (which means sexual attraction to children), depression (well, duh he would be weird if he wasn't depressed with all of this), substance abuse (alcohol,) (well that makes sense) and possibly Asperger's Syndrome (which I doubt).

As you can see, none of the diagnoses or what I call labels say a thing. They are simply words to explain what he was doing. Not one word of healing except for the fact that he can now say he was "sick" and a killer because he was "sick".

The purpose of this book is to heal the serial killer/child molester before he/she kills or kills again or molests or molests again to save their life and the lives of any future victims.

Without the explanation of why there was such a need for all the bizarre and destructive behavior and why the serial killer killed or the child molester molested there can be no healing.

It wasn't lack of Love

Jeffrey Dahmer is a good example because he was a child who was very loved by his parents. These people can come from loving, normal families and still be killers. Many of them leave their loving parents in a state of complete shock and confusion.

Couldn't tell by looking

Ted Bundy, who was considered to be the next major politician to be elected to something big, said something to the effect of, "I was 90 percent normal and 10 percent killer. Of course, he showed only his 90 percent side in his normal life.

Many have said when finding out a criminal is someone they knew, "I can't believe he did such a thing. He seemed so normal. I never would have believed it."

There are a few instances where neighbors or friends will say the person showed signs of odd behavior but most of the time there is no clue at all.

Why they feel no remorse

Here is what you may consider to be most bizarre. They feel no remorse because they did nothing wrong.

Serial killers and child molesters often or maybe it would be better said almost always, especially in the case of serial killers, feel no remorse. They feel no remorse because they feel no responsibility. They feel no responsibility because they did nothing wrong.

To them, and they have said this over and over again, they were born monsters. They were born to kill and molest. They were the worse people on the planet. They will tell you that unequivocally. They will swear to that.

They will tell you that because it is true. For as long as they could remember there was something wrong and that something wrong made them do the horrible things they did. They did not choose to be as they were. They did not want to be as they were and probably would have given anything not to be as they were as stated by Jeffrey Dahmer.

So, if it isn't lack of Love and it isn't some weirdness that was obvious and it wasn't because they wanted to hurt other people…what was it?

The missing piece of the puzzle

"I felt so completely different having to live in a world of people that were not like me." - Jeffrey Dahmer

Though psychologists understood child development and somewhat understood the stages of memory, the answer still eluded them in understanding the serial killer or child molester because they didn't have one piece of the puzzle.

This piece of the puzzle brings it all together and explains the reason there was such a powerful drive that was beyond understanding to the person and the professionals.

Without this puzzle piece you could not understand the reason for the behavior and you could not bring about a cure.

Individual Thoughts are placed in the Mind of the child in its earliest stages whether before birth or directly after to give the child the ability to perform a particular action. In each one of these Thoughts there is a Concept Thought and an Action Thought.

The Concept Thought tells what is to be done and the Action Thought does it. Every single Thought that is in the Mind has the two-part component being a Concept and Action.

It starts with a Concept Thought with the Action linked to it. "I think I can walk and I am going to do it" And this is of course done automatically without realizing it. Eventually the Concept Thought that is to walk stays the same but the Action Thought becomes the action to recall.

The Concept/Action Thought, "I know I can talk and will talk" "I know how to walk and will walk." The process becomes "I know I can talk and walk and will recall how to do so". The Action Thought is to recall. And all of this is, of course, unknown to the child and unconsciously done at the speed of lightning. After all, think of how fast a professional runner has to be thinking of how to run and remember to do so.

Let's say the Concept Thought just placed in the child is that it can purposefully move its arms and legs. The child then "realizes" that it can move its arms and legs and does so (Action Thought). That Concept is then placed in memory since the child does not have to "realize" it can move its arms and legs. It simply does so because it remembers (Action) that it can.

Each Concept Thought that is placed in the Mind of the child has to have an Action Thought connected to it. You must understand this. If a Concept Thought did not take an Action the being would know what to do but not do it. And the concept would just sit there like a book on a shelf.

Let's say the two Concept Thoughts of "you can use sound to communicate" and "you can use your words to say what you think" are placed in the child in its development to be activated at the proper time but that Concept Thought of "you can use your words to say what you think" is stopped for whatever reason. The Action Thoughts connected with both of those concepts is still trying to make it work but the one concept is stopped.

Now, you have a child whose Concept and Action Thought gives him the urge to speak. But the Concept Thought of speaking for the purpose of relaying a particular thing the child wants for itself is not working. The child will make a sound when it needs something since that part is working but it will not get out what it wants to be said. You see it often on Autistic children who want to say something and can't so they get up and walk and often make a strange noise. Sometimes they flap their hands in frustration.

There are times when the Concept Thought works perfectly but the Action Thought does not, which leaves the child incapacitated in that area. There are times when the Action Thought works perfectly but the Concept Thought does not.

To explain it better is that each individual Thought in the child's development is told "This is what you do (Concept Thought). Now do it (connected Action Thought)".

I'm sure you didn't know this but there is a disease of blindness where the person who has the disease has eyes that work perfectly. The problem either lies in the fact that the person cannot place in its Mind what it sees in its surroundings (Action Thought) or that the Concept Thought of the environment itself is not there.

The Concept Thought that what is seen relates to its surroundings is there in the first scenario but the Action Thought to use it is broken.

The person does not realize (make real using Action Thought) that what it is seeing is what is actually there in its world.   Therefore, the person is considered rightfully and by law legally blind.

In the second scenario the person has the ability to use its Concept Thought and Action Thought to see but the Concept Thought of the actual environment is missing.

In the above case of blindness, child's Concept Thought looks but does not place what it sees using the Action Thought or the Action Thought works fine but there is no prior Concept Thought of the look of the environment.

In the first scenario I liken it to a person who wants to play guitar but never picks up a guitar. The Concept Thought is there but the Action Thought is not. Therefore, the person never learns to play guitar.

In the second scenario I liken it to wanting to play a guitar but having never seen one.

In the case of this blindness Concept Thoughts and Action Thoughts which are connected would have been there from birth and were in the programming to be there as the child's "Natural State of Being" but something went wrong.

Another file in the programming is for the child to learn from cause and effect. I worked with two children who when they were born did not have this particular program working in them. They, therefore, could do nothing because they could not learn.

They just sat in wheelchairs all day until, one day a man came to work where they lived. He fed the girl by putting the bowl under her chin and shoveling the food in. She could not breathe and flailed her arms.

The Concept Thought and Action Thought took over in a desperate attempt to get air. But the Concept Thought of doing something worked and the Action Thought worked as well but the Concept Thought of what to do using her arms for a purpose like pushing the bowl away was not there.

FYI: I made sure that man never worked at that facility again.

There are many more "files" in the programming of the child tha I have previously discussed but they are too numerous to mention.

I know it's confusing but these are just examples of Concept and Action Thoughts. You just need to know that all Thoughts require Concept and Action.

So, what happened with serial killers and child molesters?

Among the numerous concepts placed in the Mind of the unborn child to be activated later is the concept of "entity" or better said "human entity". This concept has to do with existence as a human being. If you are not an "entity" you do not exist. In addition, if you do not have an "entity" you also do not have "humanity". Which is why the serial killer can kill and has to kill.

The lack of "entity" is why, I believe, Dylan Klebold wrote so often of existence and was a serial killer though it was done at once. Had he not decided to kill all at once he would have killed over years as other serial killers had done.

Serial killers need to kill in order to fill the loss of "entity" or existence. They don't hate nor do they want to hurt. They want to get what the Action Thought is pushing with a vengeance for them to have.

Child molesters and people like Russell Williams need to molest or take intimate clothing and wear it in order to fill the loss of "identity". They don't want to kill and they don't particularly want to rape either. Sometimes they do so out of anger but that is not the main goal.

In the cases of Jeffrey Dahmer and Russell Williams the Concept Thought concerning Entity and/or Identity was stopped leaving them with the Action Thought that drove them to do the horrendous things they did.

This caused them to "need" to fill that part of themselves that was supposed to be filled naturally as their "Natural State of Being".

The Concept Thought was blocked or stopped but the Action Thought was pushing with full force to make their Entity and/or Identity Concept fulfill its mission.

That need will later cause a void, the Portal and the Hell-Thought.

CHAPTER 11

In the Dark

The purpose of this chapter: to show the depth and all-encompassing nature of the situation

Now all this happened at birth and may have manifested even as early as in the first stages of development when the child is new to the world and only knows what it has been given so far.

The new born baby is obviously thinking as it stares at its new environment and the strange being that is holding it and feeding it. Therefore, the blank slate has been being filled prior to birth.

The blank slate that has been filled with Concepts is still in a kind of darkness. The darkness stays in one area in the serial killer and the child molester which is one reason why I wanted you to watch the movie Sybil and read the chapter on depth to try to understand the depth of the situation.

All of this happened in the child's earliest memory stages before birth and in the deepest part of its psyche. I can't stress that enough. Please, please watch the movie to get an idea of the depth of this situation and if you do so in the dark you will get the best understanding.

Just for your information, people can have things happen to them in the first stages of development that does not lead to loss of "identity" or "entity" in the self, no matter how awful.

If something happens in the later part of the stage of development the damage may not be as severe and there may be no loss of "entity" or "Identity" but there can still be damage and memory of why certain things are felt will not be not there.

There can be a loss of security in the first stage, causing the child to be automatically fearful and cling to its mother. There can be a loss of happiness causing the child to have a depressive situation that it cannot explain. There can be a loss of trust causing the child to be distant and suspicious.

Anger can be in the early stages with no Thoughts that lead to severe things like serial killing or child molestation because there was no loss of identity or entity.

And, of course, the cause of this anger, fear, mistrust, depression is something the person would say they have no recollection of nor would they have any idea when, why or even that it originated.

A Thought where the person has no idea why it is there is probably because it began before memory was developed.

A professor of psychology was giving a lecture where he said that for no reason whatsoever he thought of stabbing a student in the neck with a pencil. He, of course, did not stab the student. It was just a thought.

But why was the thought there? Why would he want to stab the student in the neck and was the anger actually toward that student or was the student a surrogate for another he was angry at or was he just generally angry? Or was there even anger at that particular time?

And why would one person take a thought like stabbing a person in the neck and just think it while another would bring it to fruition?

The situation, I believe, for the professor was that he was once deeply angry without knowing why which means it happened in the First Memory Stage.

But his sense of "entity" was intact not to mention common sense he didn't stab the student.

Fear can also be in the early stages making a child fearfully cling to its mother when meeting other people as a very young child. Other emotions that start in the early stages can be identified by the fact that the origin cannot be established due to lack of memory.

Jealousy, envy, fear of taking a chance, fear of being wrong and such things can begin in the early stages as well and the child may end up with unknown difficulties but the "identity" or "entity" is still there and intact.

All of these things are self-damaging but they are not the total destruction of the "entity" or the "identity" and don't lead to things that cause the void, Portal and Hell-Thought.

CHAPTER 12

The Profound Need/Severe Void and the Sucking Portal

The purpose of this chapter: To show what causes the profound drive to kill or molest.

Profound need

The Concept Thought and the Action Thought are part of one thing. They are two halves of one whole. First there is the Concept Thought then there is the connected Action Thought.

If the Concept Thought is stopped the Action Thought still fights to get that part of the psyche working. That fight causes a severe need and that need gets stronger and stronger as time goes on. There is also a void which Jeffrey Dahmer referred to as "something missing".

And this missing part is a Concept Thought. That Thought was planned to be there in the "Natural State of Being" of the person but was not placed. The Action Thought would keep pushing to make that

Concept Thought a reality. And all of what is going on is, of course, completely unknown to the being. The person will only later know something is missing and they are being driven and not know anything more.

Due to the fact that the child is "programmed" when the thing it is supposed to receive is not supplied the child NEEDS the thing it is supposed to receive and it needs it deeply. The first needs are the deepest as you can easily see in the study by Harry Harlow and the Rhesus monkeys who were deprived of love of a mother.

Please don't mistake this explanation to be saying these people were deprived of the love of the mother. Parents of serial killers and child molesters are not to blame so simply toss that concept out. This explanation is just for you to understand what the person is going through and not to blame anyone.

In that case the child does not want it. It does not desire it. It NEEDS it. And it needs it as a "Natural State of Being". It needs it as the cells of the body need air.

It is perfectly "natural" for the child to need what it is programmed to need. I can't say that enough. It is perfectly "natural" for a child to need what it is programmed to need.

Though psychologists understood child development and memory, the answer still eluded them in understanding the serial killer or child molester because they didn't have the understanding of how Concepts are implanted in the child. Nor do they understand that each concept has a Concept Thought connected to an Action Thought and that if the Concept Thought is missing the Action Thought will continue on.

This piece of the puzzle brings it all together and explains the reason there was such a powerful drive that was beyond understanding to the person and the professionals.

Without understanding this missing piece, you could not understand the reason for the behavior and you could not bring about a cure.

It is this missing piece that the Action Thought tries to get back and the drive to do so becomes severe sometimes to the point of child molestation and possibly murder.

When the whole "entity" or "identity" is completely stopped and not a concept in the Mind of the being, there is a problem and that complete loss causes the severe need and Hell-Thought and so on.

When the whole "Identity" of the person is lost at a time when the "Identity" was never recognized as existing in the first place due to lack of memory there is a severe problem.

When the whole concept of human "Entity" of the person is lost at a time when the "Entity" was never recognized as existing in the first place due to lack of memory there is a severe problem.

In math, if you take the concept that $2 + 2 = 4$ and then remove the 4 saying it is not the answer then the amount of wrong is infinite. That is why there is so much craziness in the situation and there are so many different Hell-Thoughts. When the piece that belongs is removed it leaves an opening for everything else.

Severe Void

Loveless, Empty, alone, dark, lonely, sad, detached, hopeless
Void, blank, invisible, obscure, nonresistant, nowhere, a nonbeing,
nonentity, Nothing

Oblivion, alone in the world, in despair

"The other side of the window"

A FRAME WITH NO PICTURE

There are two kinds of losses in the earlier stages of development that
can cause a person to become a perpetrator. One is the loss of Identity
and one is the loss of entity.

No matter what the person, who does not have the concept of Identity
or Entity does, it is not satisfying or it is only momentarily satisfying.
In the case of Identity loss even if, from everyone else's point of view,
he is to be admired, to him there is not even the existence of
admiration for himself. He may be happy to accomplish something
but it is superficial.

The world of a person who has lost his Identity or Entity will be like the frame without the picture. The whole concept of the personality of the being or person of the being is lost and no matter how many trumpets he learns to play or who he marries the emptiness from the loss of 'him" will still be utmost in his thought.

As with Russell Williams no matter how high he got on the ladder of success he still had the void. He still had the void and the need.

Killing will not be the main purpose of the criminal activity in the person with no Concept Thought of Identity though killing may be the end result. Killing is done as the main action by the person who has no Concept Thought of their Entity.

The lack of Entity or Identity is unimaginable.

There is a vacancy in the soul of the child, a void in the very young mind, a solitude, loneliness, aloneness, a vacuum.

The Sucking Portal

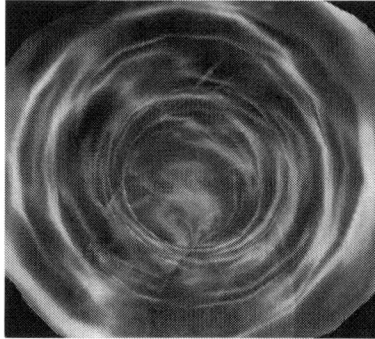

I wasn't sure if I should explain this as a door or a portal. But I soon realized that it is not a door that one walks through purposely. It is not a straight walk. It is not even a fall.

The Portal, as shown in horror movies, is a deep dark tunnel where things don't fall in but are sucked in.

Those who kill or molest are not doing nothing. They are planning, taking their time, using their money and taking life altering risks.

The loss of Entity or Identity in the perpetrator leaves a hunger; a need (Action Thought) to fulfill what should be already filled as a "Natural State of Being".

This causes the sucking portal, a drive, not a desire. It is as profound and as deep as it could possibly be and it is in the child's young psyche.

Like hunger to a starving person the need is strong and wrenching.

It sucks the child or adult in as an attempt to fill its own void or missing Concept Thought.

So, the child is left with an extreme drive, emptiness and void; an endless aching need.

The child has no idea it has this void since it started so early in the child's psyche before there was a developed memory.

The child is left with an impossible to understand and very powerful need to fill that void and has no idea that what it is feeling is due to its natural make up.

The child has no idea it is even feeling anything except a potentially extreme and insatiable need with no idea of what it is or how to fill it.

Ask yourself…do you remember before you were born?

When that need occurs the child, all of its remembered life and as it enters adulthood, tries to figure out what is happening. Sometimes it uses religion which may be why so many priests were charged with child molestation in the Spotlight investigation of 2001. Sometimes it's with drugs or a family. Sometimes it's by working nonstop. There are many ways to fill the void…or to try to fill the void.

When nothing logical works the thoughts of how to fix the problem and fill the void sometimes become very bizarre and dangerous.

But the things that many try to use to fix the problem will simply not ever work as in the cases of Russell Williams and Jeffrey Dahmer and others.

Sometimes the extremely deviant behavior does not come out until much later in the adult's life as in the case of Russell Williams who didn't start his truly deviant behavior until around forty-one years old.

Russell Williams tried and succeeded to be like Tom Cruise in Top Gun in order to fill the missing Identity and succeeded in being Top Gun. He flew planes and marched with the best of the Trenton Air Force Base. He married and owned two homes. He received tremendous respect from the highest ranking in his society. But none of that filled the void.

The void was still there and the Action Thought and the Portal was still there pulling him to try to fill the void without knowing how. And it was pulling at him because the Action Thought was doing its job trying to fill the void (making it no longer a void) which is a "Natural State of Being".

So, what happened? Russell Williams, who when asked why he did what he did and lost everything in doing so, told the investigator he had no idea as he shrugged and looked down.

Russell Williams was trapped by the need to fill the haunting void and sliding quickly down the Portal. The overwhelming powerful sucking need was overtaking him.

He needed what he was lacking so early in his life, that he didn't know was lacking, didn't know existed and couldn't obtain in any way he tried.

So sane ideas didn't work and his Mind is going at the speed of light and the need is great and the solitude is not helping. In the depth of his attempt to understand along comes a crazy wrong notion that is believed will fill the void and take away the pain and emptiness and close the Portal.

And Russell Williams and Jeffrey Dahmer who is living basically the same thing get caught in erroneous and bizarre thoughts from Hell.

Hence the term "The Portal".

CHAPTER 13
Hell-Thoughts

"Maybe the answer was out there and I would try anything to find it'- Jeffrey Dahmer

Since the Thought in the cases of Jeffrey Dahmer and Russell Williams was destructive to them and to so many and brought so many people into hell I call it Hell-Thought and feel it is appropriately named.

Before I speak about the Hell-Thought I need to explain a bit about symbolism. Hell-Thoughts are completely based on unconscious symbolic things as are many good things in our lives. A birthday card symbolizes being cared about. A smile symbolizes being liked and so on.

The eating of the person symbolized having a person as close to him as possible in the case of Jeffrey Dahmer. The symbolism of the underwear that had to be worn and not purchased in the Russell Williams case was because the underwear was intimate and as close to the person as possible and it had to be worn by both Russell and the victim in order to be part of the victim's identity which was missing in Russell.

And yes, it is all irrational because the whole situation was formed at such an early stage.

Now you have a Concept Thought that is disconnected or dormant or broken or whatever term you wish to use. And you have an Action Thought that is pushing to complete its mission of getting the Concept Thought to work.

The person or persons try everything to heal. They try getting married, having kids, flying planes, psychology, religion neuroscience and so on. Nothing of common sense works.

In their searching and contemplating in their own Mind they would think back to the time when the feeling that is causing everything was first remembered in an attempt to get answers. When they go back in time to when they would first feel it they would be in the "id" stage which one teacher called an "incredibly stupid" time in their development.

Now they are back in the time in their lives where they are "incredibly stupid" and governed by the "pleasure principal" that has no consideration for reality.

It is unconscious and impulsive. It is the pleasure only and the "I want it now" attitude. And it truly is "outrageously stupid".

One could say that the thought that, if I dress in intimate underwear that was worn by a woman to will fill my own need for whatever that need happens to be is really illogical and "outrageously stupid". And in time it shows itself as being illogical and outrageously stupid simply because the problem escalates and the solution doesn't work.

One could also say that putting one's penis in a small being who is obviously in pain and crying and who will eventually hate you and see you with disgust in order to fulfill one's need is also illogical and outrageously stupid.

One could say that to eat another person in order to fulfill one's need to be close to that person is illogical and outrageously stupid.

So why would people who would be otherwise logical do these things?

They can think illogically and irrationally and outrageously stupidly because when they are thinking about this situation they are psychologically back in the "id" stage of development of their lives. The problem first occurred in that stage of development and the loss was remembered in that same stage and to revisit the problem they are returning to the id stage and in that stage the person thinks irrationally and its thoughts are "outrageously stupid".

In order to combat what they would remember happened in the id stage the person, upon returning to that feeling, returns to that time where logic goes out the window and the person returns with a solution of what to do from that time of being "outrageous stupidity".

And remember this is all happening as the person is thinking in the void.

Upon returning from that stage in their psyche they bring with them what they think is a solution…Hell-Thought.

And remember that this thinking done in the void is deep and dark and done at the speed of lightening without any part of the thought being contemplated for logic.

If that Concept Thought is blocked or undeveloped the Action Thought will fight to get it back. In order to get it back the person believes the Hell-Thought which is that it needs to take another Entity for its own. Therefore, it kills.

Note: After Dylan Klebold gunned down as many as he could at Columbine High School and then killed himself his journals were reviewed. He spoke often in his journals of "existence" and even named his journal "existence". I find that very telling.

This is the statement made by Jeffrey Dahmer at his sentencing for the murder of 17 men and boys in February of 1992. "Your honor, it is over now. This has never been a case of trying to get free. I didn't ever want freedom. Frankly, I wanted death for myself. This was a case to tell the world that I did what I did not for reasons of hate, I hated no one."

He went on to say, "I know I was sick or evil, or both. Now I believe I was sick. The doctors have told me about my sickness and now I have some peace.

"I know how much harm I have caused, I tried to do the best I could after the arrest to make amends. But no matter what I did I could not undo the terrible harm I have caused.

I feel so bad for what I did to those poor families and I understand their rightful hate.

I decided to go through with this trial for a number of reasons. One of the reasons was to let the world know these were not hate crimes. I wanted the world of Milwaukee, which I deeply hurt, to know the truth of what I did.

I didn't want unanswered questions. All the questions have now been answered.

I wanted to find out just what it was that caused me to be so bad and evil but most of all, Mr. Boyle, I decided that maybe there was a way for us to tell the world that if there are people out there with these disorders, maybe they can get some help before they end up being hurt or hurting someone. I think the trial did that."

– Jeffrey Dahmer

Jeffrey Dahmer was not a man who wanted to hurt others. He knew at the very young age of seven that there was something seriously wrong, "something missing" but he had no idea what it was. As a child he would take dead animals and look at their organs to try to understand what was inside in order to understand himself.

Trying to get answers by looking inside a dead animal or their own body is common among those who have these issues. In my first class in abnormal psychology I saw a drawing done by a man of his arm skinned so he could see inside.

Jeffrey Dahmer wanted to tell the world that there is something out there and he wanted the people who were caught in what I call Hell-Thought to get help.

Jeffrey said that he now knows he was sick. The problem with that is that, though it is somewhat correct, the answer to what happened and why was never answered. He was told he had paraphilia. necrophilia, partialism, and other features, alcoholism, a personality disorder not otherwise specified," and an antisocial personality disorder with obsessive-compulsive and sadistic components. He was also diagnosed as having a sexual disorder not otherwise specified.

All of which means nothing. It all is simply a bunch of words with no rhyme or reason as to their existence. Along with that labeling came a lack of healing.

Jeffrey Dahmer was not an evil man. He was a man who did evil things because of a severe need that haunted him until the day he died and a Hell-Thought that caused him to kill.

The BTK serial killer, whose real name is Dennis Rader, was arrested in February of 2005. He was charged with ten counts of murder and pled guilty to all ten murders.

Rader named what he called Factor X as the cause of him having to murder as he, too, called himself a monster who could not stop. This concept of not knowing why they murder and not being able to stop ran through so many of the cases of serial killers I studied for this book.

Rader called it Factor X. We call it Hell-Thought. Another person called it a mood. Anything you call it, it is the same and it is the same for so many serial killers.

So, what specifically is a Hell-Thought?

It must be understood that all the reasons for the Hell-Thought are subtle and symbolic. Having sex with a dead body is not because the person has an attraction to bones but because the bones represent a human. Subtlety and symbolism play a huge role in the story of serial killers and child molesters.

Russell Williams stole underwear from houses around his vacation home but did not steal valuables, simply underwear and a sex toy.

Why? He could have purchased the underwear under the guise of it being for a wife or girlfriend and been completely safe. He could have purchased all he needed over the Internet. Why didn't he?

He also wore that underwear which would have been hard to do since he was quiet a large man. But he had to and had to take pictures. Why?

Why did he risk everything he had including his wife, job, dignity, rank in the Air Force and his freedom to steal underwear and sex toys from neighbors? It seems very extreme but...

Not if you understand.

Completely unbeknownst to him, Russell Williams needed what would fill the Identity void. That loss sat unconsciously in his mind in the during his childhood and into adulthood. He needed the elusive Identity that was missing from his "Natural State of Being".

He needed what would have filled the void for Identity, filled the need and stopped the void and the Portal from existing at all.

No matter how hard he tried he could not fill the void with marriage, music, success.

But his illogical way to try to fill the void was simply a Band-Aid on a hemorrhage. The erroneous thought of trying to fill the need with wearing woman's underwear can be dangerous and was and it escalated to rape and murder when it didn't work.

Underwear is very psychologically intimate. Underwear is personal and has been as close to the most intimate parts of a person as possible even sitting in the most intimate drawer. It therefore holds a special psychological place. It was in a place that was connected psychologically to a woman in his life from whom he would have gotten his Identity. His body would touch those places. They are connected to intimacy which is connected to love and Identity.

Russell Williams' Hell-Thought was…"If I put the underwear on I will have that closeness, that intimacy and therefore that love that would give me the Identity I should have had."

The problem is that didn't work because clothes and body parts still do not bring the "Identity" to the person.

But something could have.   I will explain that later.

Jeffrey Dahmer:

For Jeffrey Dahmer the story is basically the same except for the fact that his need was to kill because his void was one of Entity and he had a void in Identity as well.

The void is severe and the Portal is sucking him in and the Action Thought is fighting for the void to be filled as with Russell Williams. But there was no distraction for him as with Russell Williams. No wife, no college, no airplanes, no career, and so on. So, damage from the Hell-Thought came earlier.

Jeffrey Dahmer's Hell-Thought was that bringing someone as physically close to him as possible would fill the void left by the absent concept of Entity and stop the need and the Portal.

Therefore, his Hell-Thought is… "If I eat the person it will bring them as close to me as possible." Better said would have been, "I will have what they have. I will have their Entity" And it had to be males in his case because the unconscious part that he was missing included a missing identity as well and it would have been of a male which is a "Natural State of Being".

Jeffrey Dahmer was caught in Hell-Thought as a young man. He acted upon it to bring humans in as close to him as possible to end the void and remove the pain from the sucking Portal. But since eating people was not the answer it did not work just as with Russell Williams wearing woman's underwear did not work and the Hell-Thought as with so many others who are in prison or out did not work.

So, for Russell Williams the thought was that if I wear something intimate that meant something intimate to someone I will have them so close to me and restore my Identity and the void will be filled.

For Jeffrey Dahmer the thought was if I eat the people I will have them so close to me and they will be a part of me and I will have the Entity I lost and that will fill the void and stop the pain from the sucking Portal.

Of course, none of that would have or could have ever worked.

The Hell-Thought as unrealistic as it may be, is completely believed.

That doesn't mean it can't be removed.

So, what happens when the Hell-Thought doesn't work?

What really happens if you take the Hell-Thought and destroy it or if it doesn't work? Without removing the cause of the Hell-Thought it will simply have to be replaced with another Hell-Thought.

And, of course, even a new Hell-Thought will not work either so the situation will get worse which is what those in Criminal Science call evolving.

Evolving, due to the desire to fill the void and being unable to do so, can lead to new Hell-Thoughts.

For Russell Williams as things got worse and worse and the need was again not filled with the underwear he took and wore or the pictures he took so his need continued.

Russell Williams moved on to rape still in some way attempting to fill the void. Murder came next and it may have been simply out of necessity except for the fact that he raped women who worked on his base and with no mask and they would recognized him so he had to have been planning on murder at the start of the incident.

So, the Hell-Thought was not working and had to be changed. But that was not working either. A feeling of hopelessness must have set in.

In addition, there is a probable degrading of the person.

Just removing the Hell-Thought still leaves a void and the sucking Portal and if you add severe anger to severe hunger for relief you get disaster.

Russell Williams said that he "hoped" he would not have to do it again. Wouldn't that helplessness, hopelessness, desire for freedom from the need, degradation, lack of self-respect cause an anger?

One thing that bothered me was the fact that before he left Russell Williams wrote the message "Mercy" on the computer of a victim of the underwear stealing. He would have had to stay longer and expose himself longer to being caught. Why would he do that? Why would he take that chance?

There is no action, not a single one, that is done for no reason. None. Not one. So, why?

Since everything is done for a reason there had to be an answer to the question of why Russell Williams stopped to write on the computer.

That, for me, opened up a whole new set of questions and brought about a whole new set of answers.

Russell Williams sometimes did things to hurt as opposed to Jeffrey Dahmer who did things only out of necessity to fill the void. Even if Russell Williams had to change the Hell-Thought because the underwear situation wasn't working, as it shouldn't, and rape instead and it could have been done with more kindness as crazy as that sounds.

There was also cruelty probably caused by anger in his killing. He knew if he chose someone he knew from the Air Force Base to rape because he had to and didn't wear a mask or a condom he would have to kill the person. Also, the way he killed Jessica was very cruel.

The desire to hurt has nothing to do with the Hell-Thought and is a choice by itself.

It is well known that rape is an anger issue that has nothing to do with sex. Therefore, I believe that Russell Williams did what he did not only to fill the Hell-Thought but because he was angry.

But, why the anger?

First the person always lived on the other side of the window as Ted Kaczynski put it. So, there was from the very start a separation, isolation and a sense of being different.

Second, there was a weight that was there from the very start of the child's young life.

Third, no one understood, not even the child.

Fourth, anything that was done to counter the situation was defeated.

Fifth, the life of the criminal was overtaken by craziness over which there was no control.

Sixth, there was constant unstoppable confusion.

Seventh, there was shame and a loss of self that was severe.

Eighth, there was always the fear of getting caught.

Russell Williams and Jeffrey Dahmer at first did nothing to purposely hurt their victims. They were doing what they had to in order to fill the void. Jeffrey Dahmer was meek and mild until he died. Russell Williams, I believe, became angry when all he tried did not free him from the severe need he had and the Portal and he lashed out.

They are, in fact, ill and to be angry would make sense.

Seriously, who would have wanted to be in their shoes?

CHAPTER 14
What happened?

In the "Natural State of Being" the child has a Concept Thought linked to an Action Thought and it works perfectly unless it doesn't. The drive from the "Natural State of Being" to fulfill its mission is what causes the serial killer to have a profound need and drive to do the things that are done as a serial killer. The same is true of the child molester.

Their stories

In both instances of Russell Williams and Jeffrey Dahmer a baby was born. Some time after conception the proper preplanned set of Concept Thoughts and their connected Action Thoughts were placed in the babies Minds for them to use in their lives.

In each boy the Concept Thoughts and Action Thoughts were placed and worked as they should except for a few.

The Concept Thought and connected Action Thought for Russell Williams' Identity to be placed where it was supposed to be placed according to the preplan programming was stopped. Exactly how we do not know.

For Russell Williams the Action Thought for him to use his Identity was still intact and fighting for the Concept Thought to do what it was supposed to do concerning his Identity.

In the meantime, sort of, for Jeffrey Dahmer the Concept Thought and connected Action Thought were supposed to be placed for him to know he had a human Entity and to use it. This Concept Thought was blocked or destroyed as well and the preplaned Concept Thought that would have given him the ability to be a human Entity with all its humanistic traits was stopped. Exactly how we do not know. In addition, it may be that Jeffrey also had a block in the Identity area as well.

In both cases the Action Thoughts were working as they should have when the Concept Thoughts were placed so if all had gone as planned the Concept Thoughts would have been realized and become part of memory and they would have had their Entity and Identity

In both cases the Action Thoughts were fighting for the Concept Thoughts to do their jobs but the Concept Thoughts were unable or "missing" as Jeffrey once said.

In both cases the men could feel that there was something wrong or something missing. They tried each in their own way to figure out and cope with what was going on but to no avail.

In both cases they could feel the void and they had a desperate need to satisfy the Action Thought and remove the feeling they were feeling.

In both cases they thought about what to do and in both cases in order to do so they had to relive what memory they had of the feelings.

In both cases the thinking and trying did not work and they went back to thinking about the feeling itself. When they did they were in the "stupid" "id"stage of development.

In that stage both men were in a realm where irrationality was the norm as was incredible stupidity. But what else could they do?

Both men believed the Hell-Thought they Thought of while in that stage and both men acted upon that Hell-Thought.

Both men paid the price for acting upon the Hell-Thought and neither were healed.

Both their lives ended in disaster.

PART III

The Cure

For all the victims past and hopefully none future.

It is very important that you do not read this chapter without reading the prior chapters first. It will do you absolutely no good and may damage your chances of understanding. Please don't do that. Read the prior chapters and understand them before going on. You are worth the time. It is imperative that this be done correctly.

In addition, if you are the person seeking these answers for yourself, there is a point at which you may want to stop reading this book and seek a therapist who will walk with you through the third and fourth steps. It may be best this is done instead of you doing it alone but that is up to you. To tell the therapist why you need this procedure may not be wise but that is up to you as well.

First steps first

Before we begin, we need to talk about the Hell-Thought, which to remind you is the thought to kill or molest. The Hell-Thought, as bad as it is and as powerful as it seems, is there because something went wrong.

I need you to understand. The Hell-Thought was not there in the beginning and is not part of the actual person. It is a band-aid on a hemorrhage and we are going to heal the hemorrhage so the band-aid is no longer needed.

Since the Hell-Thought is not supposed to be there and is not part of who the person is, the Hell-Thought, for now, needs to be completely put away, completely forgotten and not thought of in any way <u>at all</u> as we go through this healing process.

Anything I talk about concerning healing will NOT include things done to accomplish the goals of the Hell-Thought because the Hell-Thought is part of the illness like a fever.

If you are the serial killer or child molester put the Hell-Thought away. This is your time. This time belongs to the child we are going to bring back.

Step 2: Choice

The healing of this disorder is done by placing the Concept Thought in the person that should have been but was not placed before birth. Because the baby would have been a blank slate when that Concept Thought was placed there would have been nothing negative to interrupt the placement of that Thought. The "Natural State of Being" would have been that the Thought was placed in a Mind that was pure.

The Thought that is being placed for healing has to do with the "Entity" or "Identity" of the person and in order for the person's own Mind to accept that Thought the person would have to be as pure as possible.

It is the choice to do one's best to gain that purity and one's work toward it that purity not whether one has corrected everything about itself but that it tried its absolute best to do so.

Once the *true* desire to see all the wrong (remember not including the Hell-Thought) and correct it in one's self has happened the person will have fulfilled a part of the requirements needed to accept the Concept Thought that was missing.

In the "Natural State of Being" when the unborn child was to receive the Concept Thought, that is now missing, that Thought was regarding an "Entity" or "Identity" that was pure. Therefore, the Concept Thought regarding that "Entity" or "Identity" has to be pure to be accepted.

It is the *true desire* in the heart of the person not the actual fixing of little things that make the person pure as required by the "Natural State of Being" to accept the missing Concept Thought.

If the choice is made to wholeheartedly see what needs to be seen and do what needs to be done then move on and heal. If not, don't waste your time reading on because you will not accept your own "Entity" or "Identity" and you will not be able to fill the void with the Concept Thought it should have had in the first place.

If you are willing to do what needs to be done let's move on and build the rest of the child.

Step 3: Get rid of the garbage. See only the bad in you for now.

When doing this you will be looking at the 90% Ted Bundy spoke of as the normal person not the 10% serial killer. But the actions that were taken during the Hell-Thought ***but not due to it because it is an illness*** have to be included. An example would be rape done out of anger or vengeance during a murder that was done to fulfill the Hell-Thought.

In Alcoholics Anonymous they call it a 4th step. In other organizations they call it other things. But what has to be done is "a fearless and searching moral inventory". Fearless because fear will block the truth, searching because it takes work, lots of time and in-depth examination of past behavior and motives; and moral because the bad has to be seen.

Here is why it needs to be done:

The person that was being built Thought by Thought before birth was pure because the person was new. There was no jealousy, vengeance, hate and so on. It was just a brand-new person.

The child can receive the Concept Thought of its human "Entity" and accepts its "Identity" when those Concept Thoughts are first placed in the Mind of the child because there is no history of any kind and certainly no history that would make it reject its "Entity" or "Identity". The Concept Thoughts are being placed on a blank slate.

Negative or bad things in the person's thought have to be removed (not regarding the actual acts of killing or molestation because that is illness). The "Natural State of Being" will not accept as its "Entity" or

"Identity" someone who is bad in their thinking because it is not natural. It was not the child's "Natural State of Being" and it will be rejected or automatically blocked.

David Berkowitz, who had been in prison for decades for killing six people, once said that "Prison is a place of reflection and self-examination where a man is forced to come to terms with himself."

For David Berkowitz self-examination was required. He had been in prison for 22 years of a life sentence when he gave the testimony that I ran across on YouTube.

The first decade or so after he was caught, he played all the mind games he could to get free from prison. He said a dog told him to do it and so on.

He took actions so he could give the right answers to psychiatrists. And he said in the interview on YouTube that he was "just parroting back to them what they wanted to hear.

But removing the enabling defense mechanisms or manipulation concepts or the revenge concepts, in other words, the crutches that blocked the Truth freed him to begin to heal.

In prison there is no one to hear you and no one to care. Except for God and your own Thoughts, you are on your own. And you are on your own for a long, long time, maybe for your entire life.

The manipulation tactics of lying about why he killed and the things he did that were bad began to show for what they were. More than anything lying to himself was beginning to change to being truthful to himself.

So, his own responsibility for the things he did that had nothing to do with the actual Hell-Thought were beginning to come to light and be understood and accepted.

The lies, the manipulation and the selfishness of David as a person were uncovered and were dissolved. That left him simply a person who was a bad person who knew he was a bad person.

The person has to remove the garbage to rebuild the "Entity" and/or "Identity" as it was originally meant to be with no obstacles.

You may want to note that in the case of loss of "Identity", physical things that a person would consider to be offensive can play a part in causing bad feelings about the self. In order for healing to occur all things have to be looked at even the negative things that are physical and they need to be accepted or even liked if that is possible.

Forgiveness plays a big part as well so when you see and change, forgive as well. That will complete this part of the healing.

possible not probable

A person can say, "From this day forward I will be the person I was meant to be". The person can examine from this moment forward each thing that the person does and make sure it is based on the deepest Love and Truth or good in whatever terms you want to use. That is possible.

Knowing now what caused the person to lose themselves in the first place may facilitate a complete change where the person could say they are totally different in the deepest part of their soul and the "band-aid Hell-Thought" is not only no longer needed and no longer has power but is actually seen as what it is which is unreal and illogical. That is possible.

That change would have to be absolute and complete with a full heart where the old person and every single one of that person's bad traits is completely gone and replaced. But that is rare and most often self–examination of the things in the person's life is required and in my opinion is highly recommended.

Step 4: See only the good.

If you have chosen to look at and eliminate all the negative, then you should be a blank slate standing naked and alone but clean.

Now you have to look back in your life and see only the good. Just as you did with the searching moral inventory do it again only see the good you have done in your life.

Take time to do it and look at every… little… thing… no matter how small and put that in a data bank because this is what you really are. This is the beginning of the building of the real person.

Fill that data bank with everything you can remember. Write down every thing no matter how small that would be a good thing you did. Write down things even if you were going to do good but did not get the opportunity.

Write down physical talents and traits as well including jokes, music, math, art, hair color, great hands, great feet. Write down everything good about you and make it a long list.

Remember to look at motive since that shows the true good.

Step 5: Integrating the Entity or Identity back into the child

This was the hardest part of the whole book. How do we put the genie back in the bottle?

It was so hard figuring out how to do this.

Until I realized how Sybil did it.

Now you have a person in front of you. You know this person. You took all the previous steps and you know the former bad, you know the choice that was made and you know the good that is its "Natural State of Being". What now?

It needs to be stated that just the understanding of what happened alone can be a cure. It sheds light into the darkness and makes the thought of killing or molesting something that is understood and not hidden to come out later with a vengeance.

In addition, understanding what happened that caused the Hell-Thought and seeing the aspects of the person both good and bad along with the choice to do good to be able to integrate can also be a cure in itself.

Love and Changing the Thought

Let's start with Love

The child's "Natural State of Being" includes togetherness and unity and so much more.

From conception the egg lands on a soft billowy substance in the uterus. That soft billowy substance is its home for the first nine months of its life.

In its "Natural State of Being" it floats in perfectly planned ninety-eight-degree warm water and sits in billowy softness being fed continually through its mother. In its preplanned environment the child lives in a world of Love.

The child, from the very beginning swims in a world of warm water and loving softness being continually fed not only physical nutrition but Thought Concepts all of which are based on and include Love.

All are for the purpose of Loving the child.

In my studies I realized something that surprised me. The Concept Thought of being Loved is *not* placed in the child. Every Concept Thought placed in the child is done with and for Love and the child feels that Love unknowingly and automatically.

There is not an individual Thought placed in the child that it is Love. Love is a part of every single Thought placed in the child. I can't tell you how important that is.

Changing the Thought

David Berkowitz decided to look at his own actions that damaged his life and to do so honestly no matter the pain. When he did that, he took the third step (or in Alcoholics Anonymous the 4th step). A priest talked to him about being God's child and being valued and loved no matter what. When he accepted that he was God's child he automatically accepted that he was a human entity. At that moment he put the genie back in the bottle or better said he put the Thought that he was a human "Entity" and moreover as loving human "Entity" back into his consciousness.

The Hell-Thought was gone. The statement in the video was…As far as the old David is concerned: "It's like another life that I don't ever recognize any more."

Integration:

It took me many days of mindboggling work and many days of headaches and sleeping long hours to recover to finally fill in this one gap that seemed more like the Grand Canyon. How do we put the genie back in the bottle? How do I lead you to cross that bridge to integration and healing?

If you don't follow the same path as David and the process doesn't come automatically after understanding, how do you purposely put the genie back in the bottle or the Thought back in the Mind?

You put the Thought back in the Mind by taking the action to do so.

We put Thoughts in our Minds all the time. We think, "I'm upset so I have to eat and eat" or "My girlfriend/boyfriend doesn't love me, I must be nothing."

So, what is the actual Concept that needs to be added?

Concerning the person who kills, if the child was just a being that is fed Thought Concepts that were used for it to grow it would be no different than a computer or a robot and we would live in a world where we were separate from each other and simply existing.

In the serial killer, mass killer or random killer the Concept Thought that is missing is that of human "Entity" which is a *contained thinking, living part of the being whose sole purpose is to express love.* As real as the heart to pump blood, this "Entity" has the job of expressing love which makes it human.

If this human "Entity" is missing it makes it not only easier to kill but desired to the point of wanting to take the human "Entity" from anyone it can for itself.

In the case of Jeffrey Dahmer filling this missing human "Entity" was done by eating another person thereby taking their "humanity". Since that, of course, didn't work he tried it over and over again making him a serial killer. The killing is always done to take the person's humanity.

Child Molestation is done to take the person's identity.

I thought I would explain how the process works to fill or change a Concept with I thought I would use of the story of Sybil Dorsett who had Multiple Personality Disorder or DID Dissociative Identity Disorder.

Sybil

Due to severe trauma Sybil's mind separated her personality into sixteen separate personalities she believed to be actual selves with each holding a specific thing. One held anger, the other held her music, the other her childhood and so on. The Concept believed, though unknowingly and unconsciously by her because of memory being undeveloped, was that there were multiple "selves" but in actuality they were sections of the same "self".

After years of therapy which included at times Sybil simply sitting on Dr. Wilbur's lap for love and comfort, she decided it was time to "integrate" her personalities which actually meant to eliminate the Concept of there being multiple "selves" and accept the Concept of there being one "self" with multiple facets.

After the hard decision to integrate, meeting each one at a time Sybil was told what the personality traits were of each one or what the job was of each one. This one held your anger, this one held your paintings, this one held your music and so on.

Sybil looked at every one of the personalities that were a part of herself and embraced it, acknowledged it, loved it and accepted it as part of her being. The person with the disorders in this book will have to do somewhat the same. They have to look at themselves and accept their being or their identity as well.

Sybil had to consciously take the action to change her Thought.

The person with the child molestation disorder in this book has to embrace the conglomerate of traits that form the contained and unique "Identity" of the contained thinking, living being that is them.

Those with "Entity" disorder have to embrace the self they have examined, as Sybil did her personalities, as an actual contained thinking, living part of the being whose sole purpose is to express love.

For sybil it was a change of Thought, for the killing person or molesting person it is a placement of Thought.

It was that acceptance of the person of Sybil by Sybil that changed the introduction into an integration.

It needs to be a conscious action of the person to accept either the "Identity" or the "Entity" of the being they are for them to heal.

David did it unknowingly so it can be done.

Why did this happen to me or my loved one?

Let's go back to the building of the child. Scientists say there are over 37 trillion cells in the human body. Each of the physical cells is given an instruction and each has to work in unison with other cells. The plan is perfect and set but the unborn baby is now in the "world" and things go wrong as any gynecologist or prenatal doctor can tell you. The plan is perfect but once in the material world, things can and often do go wrong.

Frankly, I'm surprised at the number of things that go right in the body considering how complex it is and how it has to work as a whole.

How much can go wrong when that many cells and their Thoughts are placed in the body? Babies are born with cleft palate, hammer toes and some with birthmarks and some with achondroplasia, some with heart defects, and the list goes on and on. Physically things go wrong and they are seen when the child is born.

Now let's look at the cognitive things, the Thoughts that are placed in the Mind to be used with the body. Are there hundreds of thousands of Thoughts or are there millions or trillions as with the cells of the body? No matter what the actual number, there are a lot of Thoughts placed in the Mind of the unborn child before birth and though the plan is perfect, things can go wrong.

For some what goes wrong physically is no big deal and does not affect the child's life like webbed toes or undeveloped pinky fingers. But for some what goes wrong physically is major and can affect even whether child lives or not and what condition it would live in.

The same is true of the Thoughts placed in the Mind of the child. For some what goes wrong mentally is no big deal and does not affect the child's life like my spatial disability that gave me a horrible sense of direction and the inability to hang a picture straight. But for some what goes wrong mentally is major and can affect whether a child lives a normal life or is schizophrenic or autistic and so on.

So, why did this horrendous thing happen to you or your loved one? It happened for the same reason a clubbed foot or heart condition happened to another unborn child. It happened because we live in a material world and that is what happens in a material world. In other words, shit happens.

ENJOY:

If you are the person healed from the information in this book, now you are live in the world with the rest of us and are no longer on the "other side of the window" so enjoy your new world. Feel the wind in your face and know it was put there for you. Feel the cool refreshing feeling of a cold glass of water. Taste the food you are eating as if you were never able to taste food before. Look at the beautiful hair on a person, black, red, yellow and brown. Look at eye color. Think of the fur of a kitten that was there for you to feel. Look at comical things like animals and comedians whose comedy is a gift. Hear sounds as if you had never heard them before. Feel fabrics or animals or grass. Listen to the birds.

See all of it. Every day see more and more. And when you realize that there is so much and all those things were purposely put there for you, for us, then you will realize how Loved you are and will feel Loved more than the way the rest of us feel Loved because we have become accustomed to it.

The Cough in the Living Room that lit up my world:

I wanted to share a story with you of Love and my mother who was the beautiful shining light of my childhood in so many ways.

I wanted to share with you a time when my feeling of extreme sadness and degradation suddenly changed in an instant and made it obvious to me how a Thought could change a person's world.

I was not brought up with any religion whatsoever but I always felt Loved and I Loved others very much as well as you should be able to tell by this book.

I did not have a loss in my earlier development so I had no void. But I did know what it is like to feel belittled and then have that horrible feeling simply wiped away.

When I was younger, about 12 years old, I was in the company of someone for quite a few hours who was abusive. He dumped my purse. He was physical. It was cruel and belittling.

I was supposed to be in the care of someone who loved me and would protect me but that person, unbeknownst to my mother who would have had a fit, went to the movies leaving me in the company of this hurtful person. That person who left me to go to the movies was my father.

When I got home to my mother I went to bed. As I lay there, I was acutely aware of the feeling of being worthless that I had gotten from being left by my father who saw me little and instead went to a movie and degraded by someone I wanted to like me. To this day I have not forgotten that feeling.

I lay in my bed looking up at the stick-on stars on my ceiling that I always loved I realized that even they looked different.

Then the most wonderful thing happened. My mother, who I knew Loved me as a mother should, did something that was so common but that had a profound effect on me.

She coughed.

As she sat in the living room right down the hall she simply coughed.

But her cough lit up my room.

After being in the company of someone who was so awful, my mother coughed in the living room and changed it all.

In an instant the room that was so dark and cold lit up with light and warmth. The feeling of inferiority and worthlessness, that feeling as I looked at the stick-on stars on the ceiling, disappeared as the darkness disappears to light.

It was simply gone.

The cough reminded me of how Loved I was by the person coughing in the living room. It was a remarkable experience.

I sat up in bed in the now warm room and looked at my beautiful stars and my beautiful room and thought of what had just happened to me as I enjoyed the feeling of being Loved.

Then a tremendous sadness came over me. "What happens to those who don't have anyone to cough in the living room?" I thought.

"What happens to them?"

That was my great story of the power of Love to change dark into light and a tribute to my wonderful mother whose love and education led me to be able to write this book.

This book is a labor of Love for whoever needs it. I hope at the end of this book when you realize the healing and take the steps to make it happen, that you will be able to laugh at the man who yells at you from his car and Love as the mother sitting in the living room.

That is my hope.

ALL…everything that I understand, I only understand because I love."

Leo Tolstoy

The following pages include references that were added for those who need additional information and for those who need a diagnoses in the psychology field.

PSYCHOLOGY AND REFERENCES

FOR THOSE WHO NEED TO HEAR IT THROUGH THE TERMS OF PSYCHOLOGY:

I absolutely hate labels. Many times they are just words that describe the problem with no solution. Psychiatry also often leaves out Thought which is bizarre because everything in caused by Thought.

If you absolutely, positively have to go this route, which I hope you don't, this is the way. But please, please you don't need to use it.

Since psychiatry needs labels I would label this situation as such:

DISSOCIATIVE ENTITY DISORDER/ DISSOCIATIVE IDENTITY LOSS DISORDER

The healing of the serial killer is mostly the same as the healing of the child molester and both can be likened to the healing of those with multiple personality or currently called Dissociative Identity Disorder (DID).

A person with Multiple Personality Disorder or Dissociative Identity Disorder once said that she manufactured a personality to fit her particular situation. Likewise, the serial killer and the child molester through the Hell-Thought have manufactured an answer to suit the particular situation but did so because they had no choice to try something and common sense did not work.

In the Multiple Personality DID disorder the true Thought that there was a single entity being called the "self" was replaced with the

130

erroneous Thought that the "self" instead of being one being with many facets was many beings.

With the serial killer the true Thought that the being is a contained thinking, living, loving entity, in other words, a human was replaced with the "self" being completely removed.

In the case of the child molester the true Thought that this is your identity and you like it because it is you is replaced with the Thought no identity at all or one that is completely unknowingly rejected.

This is the reason the name I choose for the disorder has the word "loss" in it. It is not that it was changed as much as nothing replaced it. Therefore, it left a severe hole.

In the Multiple Personality (DID) disorder there was a replacement. The one 'self' was replaced with many selves. With those who are serial killers and child molesters there was no replacement.

Therefore, I have named the disorder for the serial killer Dissociative Entity Loss Disorder or DELD. Dissociative because the being is disconnected from its origin, Entity because the disconnect was in the Thought of what the Entity was made to be, Loss because the Entity was lost and Disorder because it is a disorder.

I named the disorder for the child molester and similar behavior Dissociative Identity Loss Disorder or DILD. Dissociative because the being has dissociated from its origin, Identity because the disconnect was from the natural concept of accepting the image of the self... of the being, Loss because the Identity was lost because it happened so early and Disorder because it is a disorder.

Healing the patient with Multiple Personality Dissociative Identity Disorder is done through integration of the perceived separate personalities into the Truth that the being is actually one multifaceted personality. Just like the Multiple Personality DID person those with serial killer or child molester disorders must be integrated with what the original concept of the being as it was before the dissociation or loss. See previous pages on healing.

In DID the main goal is for the person to realize and live the fact that there is only one "self" and all the other "selves" are really parts of the main self. In order to do that the person would have to understand the different personalities and their role in the story. Then, the DID person could be introduced to them when the person is ready to do so.

The main goal in serial killer is for the person to see and make real its place in the world as a human entity.

The main goal of child molester is for the person to accept its identity as its one and only flawed but liked "self".

The basic goal is to return the person to its "Natural State of Being" which is the being that it was planned to be before the dissociation or loss happened.

FYI: The fugue state that is in the Multiple Personality is different from the behavior fugue state that is in the serial killer and the child molester. The fugue state in the Multiple Personality has an amnesia connected to it. The behavior fugue state in serial killers and child molesters has no amnesia and the act is completely remembered by the person.

REFERENCES:

David Berkowitz YouTube Video: A Look Back: Son of Sam Says God Leads

Child Development/Piaget:

For this book, in the area of child development, I mostly used the research of Piaget. He was a Swiss clinical psychologist who was known for his pioneering work in Child Development and genetic epistemology, which is the study of how knowledge structures work This was fascinating to me.

He studied how children form their knowledge structures in the world. He researched and studied the origin of things concerning the child's growing mind.

Jean Piaget studied the origin of the cognitive (mental learning) process that made the child develop into an adult. His research brought about, for me, the understanding of the depth and progression of the growing Mind of the child and his research proved true and usable in my classroom.

To this day I admire him for his remarkable research and work.

Piaget realized and recorded things concerning cognitive development in the child that have proven to be true and have worked time and again in my career in working with the most severe of behaviorally or cognitively handicapped students. Because of this proof, I call it not a theory but a fact, an answer.

Piaget was one who discovered the Stages of Thought progression in cognitive development and recorded and named them. One of the Concept Thoughts that Piaget discussed was formed in the stage he called the Sensorimotor Stage. This stage is from 0-2 years of age. In this stage he says that the child learns "that they exist separately from the objects and people around them".

Love/Harry Harlow

It was believed many years ago that the child's Love was not Love at all but simply a primitive desire to be fed. But along came a man named Harry Harlow who destroyed that belief.

Though his experiments were not on humans and probably shouldn't have been done on monkeys either they destroyed a wrong belief and reinforced a correct one.

Harry Harlow removed baby monkeys from their mothers at a very young age and replaced the mother with either a cloth mother, a wire mother and a mother that had a bottle of milk attached.

The baby monkey went for the soft mother first and mostly going only to the mother with the bottle to eat and back to the soft mother.

Harlow called his experiments and findings experiments in Love.

The monkey that runs to the cloth mother because the Action Thought tells it to in order to fill the Concept Thought that it is Loved is no different in purpose than the serial killer who runs to fulfill its Action

134

Thought to kill or the child molester who runs to fulfill its Action Thought to molest.

There is also a Concept Thought in the program of the child for the child to need to be held or cuddled by something soft as seen in the monkey experiments of Harry Harlow and it needs to be noted that Harlow's experiments show the attachment had nothing to do with feeding. It is an attachment to warmth and softness which would be Love.

Memory/Freud:

Though I am not a Sigmund Freud fan and think much of what he said was not accurate I believe his memory/morality research was accurate and used it. He called his sections the Id, Ego and Superego.

Thought/Mary Baker Eddy

There is so much to say here that you will have to look it up yourself if you choose to know more.

19519050R00086

Printed in Great Britain
by Amazon